The Book of Jeremiah

Also by Beatriz Copello and published by Ginninderra Press
Witches, Women & Words
No Salami Fairy Bread
Rambles

Beatriz Copello

The Book of Jeremiah

The Book of Jeremiah
ISBN 978 1 74027 246 9
Copyright © text Beatriz Copello 2024

Cover image: Loana Sinaga

First published 2024 by
Ginninderra Press
PO Box 2 Bentleigh 3204
ginninderrapress.com.au

Foreword

In her new, intriguing 'cli-fi' work, Beatriz Copello gives us almost Biblical-like verses. With deep insight into environmental, feminist and political concerns, she proves her poetic skill once more. We follow Jeremiah, called The One, reborn in Epinaster, a harsh settlement created after multiple disasters have ravaged the earth: *It was the age of ages / it was the age of wars / it was the age of pain when everything was turned to grey powder that /choked humans and beasts /...only the silence left.*

To escape the domination of The Code Keepers, he journeys to find his humanity and to love freely: *I suffer/I cry/ I want to be a whole man.* After many tribulations, he finds the truth about the the past in books hidden in a cave, and meets Graha, a woman he can truly love: *I want to plait her hair /and run my hands /on the contours of her body.* She tells him *...I love you like the bats love dark nights...like the locust love grasses.* With his new knowledge, he plots a revolution against The Code Keepers, urging: *...knowledge will destroy our apathy...books are not evil, books are children of the brain...let's seek freedom as we seek mushrooms.*

With echoes of her powerful poetry collection 'Witches, Women & Words, Copello has created a prescient work of great imagination – a disturbing world described in compelling verses, a world we can gasp at and learn from.

Pip Griffin

Contents

Characters	9
Words	10
Places in the Land of Epinaster	11
The Code	12
In His Previous Life Jeremiah Played His Lyre	13
Jeremiah Sealed the Fate	15
On Jeremiahs Third Incarnation	16
The Cursed One Grows and Leaves	18
Jeremiah Reflects	19
The One Who Knows All	20
Jeremiah's Harvest	21
The Parable of Pigeon Shit	22
The Notebook	24
Rescuing His Heart	25
Jeremiah Sings to Life	27
Full Moon	28
Jeremiah Crossed the Desert	30
The Gone Days	34
Jeremiah Was in the Dream of the Chaotic Minds	36
Life in Epinaster	37
Humans	38
Graha	39
Versing in the Mind	41
Jeremiah and Camus	42
The Genius and the Laurels	43
Feeling	44
No Light	45
The Woman	46
Famine	47

Jeremiah at the Edge of a Mountain	48
Graha's Hold	49
Respect	51
Graha's Prayer by the Lake	52
Pasodoble	53
Planning the Revolution	58
Jeremiah Asks the Pigeons For Their Blessing	59
The Pigeons Advise	60
The First Speech of Jeremiah	61
Graha Escapes	63
The Stone	64

Characters

Jeremiah: main character.
The Woman: Jeremiah's ex-lover.
Kelot: Jeremiah's mother, also a witch.
The Pigeons: evolved pigeons, they rescued Jeremiah and brought him up.
The Witches: they have been expelled from Turoa and live in the Forbidden Lands. The witches defy all rules and have books and artefacts.
Damora: a warlock.
Graha: Jeremiah falls in love with her.
The Mutants: people with deformities due to chemical and atomic wars.
The Pures: humans who did not inherit deformities that were the result of the impact of chemical and atomic weapons.
The Evolved: the Pigeons
The Great Code Keeper: reigns with a group of his friends and they control and set the rules.

Words

Truna: money used in Epinaster.
Cretonis: a drug to maintain erection and stop people from falling asleep.

Places in the Land of Epinaster

Maratuja Desert: some tribes live there.
Turoa Village: Graha lives there.
Tetoo Village: important people live there.
Untar Village: the mutants live there.
The Forbidden lands: the Witches live there.
Madura Mountains
Mountain of Pigeon Shit
Pine Forest
Dead Lake No Fish
Tewan River
Oruja Caves: Jeremiah was told by the Pigeons that in the cave there was a library, notebooks and artefacts. He lives in the cave.

The Code

The Great Code Keeper reign supreme together with his team the Code Keepers.

Rules are only set by the elected Pures.

Every human must respect this code.

There is no room for thinking machines in the new society.

No machine will take the place of human hands.

No woman will remain a virgin after the start of the red floods.

Men must deflower as many virgins as they can since procreation is an imperative of the New Society.

To abort is a crime. Witches who perform abortions will be killed.

Witches are not allowed in Epinaster.

The dead must be returned to the Earth except those who break the Code and are burnt.

Anyone found with a book must be stoned and be offered to the sacred river.

Parents are to discourage new thinking in children.

No new Gods are to be created.

In His Previous Life Jeremiah Played His Lyre

It was the age of ages
        it was the age of wars
                it was the age of pain.

Times in which an error
lasted for many years
times of obsolete stammers.

It was then that
Jeremiah returned
        playing his lyre.
He was searching
for a rational explanation.
He walked alone
by the crevices
of a fraudulent plan.

The Irrationals were
        blind to cruelty
                sorrows and death.

He bedded an illusion
he dreamt of peace
he dreamt of freedom.
…and the war commenced.

Everything collapsed
under the rickle of deceit
amoral doctrine
which flaunted words
pretending to be
God given.
Injured in battle
with scorn
he prepared to depart,
while suspended
from a thin string
his heart swung
among the innocent.
Jeremiah close is eyes
he smiled and believed
there was still life
in his injured body.

Jeremiah Sealed the Fate

To provoke the old and tired credulity
Jeremiah rescinded of all illusions
he hid his spirit and wasted his strength.
Entrenched in past reality
and faithful to the dead
he fought the enemy, who merciless,
forced him to offer his weak flank.
Jeremiah wore his doubts
like a pauper wears his rugs
and cried for peace in a useless war.
Some wanted to build a wall
to hide the truth and the suffering,
as they devoured each other.
Others wanted to see the long corridor
that led to the Chaotic Minds who plan
and control the Future. Some
rebelled and continued fighting.
Jeremiah gave himself up,
 immolated he laughed.
He knew he would return
to a destroyed world.

On Jeremiahs Third Incarnation

The Birth

The witch screamed and cursed
at the bastard child she did not want.
On her knees, hands trembling
she pulled at the infant's legs
who dropped onto the burning sands
of the Maratuja desert.
The Woman, known as Kelot
read pigeons' entrails at the market,
no secrets for the town's witch,
but her pregnancy: a mystery
many believed Damora had entered her
on the 'Night of no Pigeons'
when evil spirits roam the land.

The Curse

Kelot buried the child
under a pile of leaves
and said as she spat,
'I curse you, never
will you be the one
that you want to be.
Die Damora's shit.'

The Pigeons

The birds which have
promised faithfulness to
The Uncertain Future
disobeyed the orders,
'No interference
in human affairs' but
they had a rebel spirit.

The Rescue

The Pigeons saw
Kelot's deed and
with a flutter of wings
they rescued the child.
In a hollow tree trunk
he was placed, fed
cared for and taught.
The Pigeons hummed arias
that no evil or harm
befall on 'The One'.
Jeremiah grew
orphan of love
but not of reason and sense.

The Cursed One Grows and Leaves

Ready to drink the juices
of life and love
Jeremiah left The Pigeons,
at the edge of the desert
and went to live
in the Oru Caves.
As he was leaving
The Pigeons shouted, 'Find
meaning and purpose.
Don't forget us.'

Jeremiah Reflects

What is this heaviness
that crushes my heart?
Black ocean of torments
that shakes my body,
celestial debris igniting
my cells, my body…
this part of me
that craves 'something'
as the Maratuja's people
thirst for water.
The Pigeons had preached me,
'Reject the flesh!' But why?
I reflect on the lesson
as I rub my sex with wet moss.
An in vain act, as this enduring pain
consumes my brain
like anthrax consumes skin.'

The One Who Knows All

Jeremiah cried and his tears
as they fell watered the mushrooms
a delicacy which when eaten
opens the eyes to new worlds
chiaroscuro places of beauty
regale of the gods. In evil cities
it sells for 500 Trunas an ounce.

Jeremiah's Harvest

It was harvest time when Jeremiah
dreamt of a new world
dreams which like kites flu into space.
He slept and woke up in pain,
his sex burnt with a fire like
the ones that clean the land
of stubble before planting the seed.
He went in search of maidens,
deflowering had become an obsession.
With his head down he walked
through a forest where he saw
a book he had lost a long time ago,
it was opened on page 33.
Jeremiah half closed his eyes
to read, 'It is ignominious
to corrupt virgins in the morning.'
Jeremiah cursed and sat on a rock
he swayed his body as he masturbated.

The Parable of Pigeon Shit

Jeremiah, the man, the soul, The One with no identity left his world to enslave himself in the mind of a woman: the Woman. She knew he was her prisoner, she humiliated and tortured him. Metaphorically she had taken his eyes out and cut out his tongue. Yet…she said she loved him. He could still see and tasted and his tongue drew rainbows on maidens' breasts.

Jeremiah

Jeremiah recognised his errors
and abandoned The Woman.
He enveloped himself in shame
and dragged his feet across
a desert. He stopped.
and for an era, he cried.
His tears formed a lake
where the blameless came to bathe.
Jeremiah made love to them,
after they played and danced
while a murder of crows
sang to the uncertain future
behind a mountain
of pigeon shit.

The Woman

In a box the Woman kept
Jeremiah's heart. She knew
he would return to reclaim it.
Angst and fatigue
dressed her days. Waiting
she laid her boredom
in the pages of Kafka's
The Judgement.

The Notebook

After going walkabout in the Madura Mountains
Jeremiah returned to live amongst the men and women
of this callous present. He wrote in his notebook,
'The need to dream has been firmly tied
to the chariot of madness, prostituted ambition
of imperfect beings, unequal sensations,
centurions in search of adventures.'
The One found himself in a wasted and tired land
where reason was split into segments. He searched for the truth
behind a mask which mirrored his own face.
He confronted, the quasi-erotic desire to live for the sake of living,
'Life, ephemeral and soothing gives them
the exact measure of that which in vain departs,'
he wrote in his tattered and dirty notebook.
In order to provoke the old and wasted credulity
Jeremiah shed futile illusions and hid his demoralised spirit.

Rescuing His Heart

On the way to the Maratuja desert lived the Woman
who had Jeremiah's heart, and he pondered
as he chewed his daily ration, 'Shall I rescue my heart?'
He wanted to love again, to enter a woman
just because he loved her. He was tired
of deflowering virgins to get rid of their blight*
this was as hard as it was to convince the pigeons
to stop attacking the Uncertain Future.
The young man wrote in his tattered notebook,
'I will get my heart back,' and departed.
After three moons he arrived at the Woman's cave
he shouted, 'Life is not living without you!'
On hearing Jeremiah's voice, the Woman ran to him
slapped him twice and then embraced him.
In preparation for his plan he had drunk
the juice of cretanis known for its ability
to give sexual power and prevent sleep.
On the dirt ground they made love for the remains of the day
Night found them still on the ground, murmuring
words of passion and desire. Morning brought
renewed energies but finally the Woman exhausted
entered the world inhabited by gods, spirits and demons.

Desperate to find his heart he searched the cave for hours –
found the box and furiously threw it to the ground.
The box broke and amongst the pieces the crystal heart shone.
He took the enchanted object which the Woman,
with the aid of demons had used to gain his love.
He filled the deer bladder with water and left the Woman forever.

*There is a story around the village that says that the Woman slept
for one hundred days and when she realised the heart was gone
she never slept again.*

---

* In Jeremiah's land for a woman to be a virgin after fifteen years of
age was considered a grave sin.

Jeremiah Sings to Life

The score of life, mysterious music
teaches us to love and to hate but also to forget.
We travel with heavy burdens and insecurities,
sometimes we find solace carrying the grief
 of those who like us walk aimlessly.
Death dressed with the shawl of patience
sighs and waits knowing that
we will end in her eternal bosom.
Pretending she is not there I live
and like a poor donkey, carry
on my fragile shoulders my sorrows,
while acid hunger corrodes my stomach
and loneliness carves a hole in my mind,
my emotions are withered flowers
my passion just a fantasy.

                                                I suffer
                                                  I cry
                                I want to be a whole man

The Pigeons with tenderness
peck my hand and murmur in my ear,
'You are what you think…
Step by step, with valour and dignity
follow a new road and day-by-day, raise your eyes
to the once blue sky as the legend tells us.'
I imagine its beauty and promise to be the one I want to be.
The crumbs on my plate I devoured with delight
and will let myself be involved in crazy passions,
furious as stormy nights in the month
when the frogs croak and the lakes fill with froth.
Death waits for me, but I don't care…I live.

Full Moon

Jeremiah

He is her prisoner. She commands and he obeys.

The woman

She created a world, a sombre place of decay and pain
where a sour taste lingers in the mouth:
absent solace, unburied crisis.

Jeremiah

He writes poems for her in the hope that she frees his heart.
The Woman never hears his words, which she considers are
pedantic syllogism.

His Poem

Let me make you
a necklace of spume
to adorn your body
I will take you
flying on a red kite
we'll be flamingos
amidst clouds.

The woman

She created him god-like, but he metamorphosed into a
being who laughs at her mistakes and her nonsensical sexual
fantasies.

Her Poem

My entrails are paper-thin
as the hope of peace
on the edge of war
I am a used stamp
on a discarded envelop.
Is the face on the stamp
the face in the mirror?
Do I exist or did he create me?

Jeremiah

He patiently waits, meditates and makes plans. Always 'the notebook' is by his side during the pilgrimage into her mind, but it is her body that moves him.

His poem

I want to plait her hair
and run my hands
on the contour of her body
febrile my desires.
Rivulets of beings
conundrums of souls
clashing minds
no resolution.
The woman
She also sleeps.

Jeremiah Crossed the Desert

Failure was his curse
every project, every plan
disintegrated like badly fired
earthen pottery. Nearly ready
to succumb to his failures
he went to The Pigeons
to seek their advice.
'Find your mother,
and ask for the curse to be lifted,'
The Pigeons cooed and flapped
their wings pointing to the north.
Jeremiah asked who was the woman
that had given birth to him.
'Find the blonde witch, in the Maratuja,'
said the birds. Jeremiah cooed back
to thank the parents who had
brought him up, fed him
seeds, earthworms,
insects and snails.
Jeremiah, before departing
collected water in the bladder of a deer
and cooked lentil bread for the long trip.

The Maratuja desert welcomed him
with a storm of sand and a cloud of locusts,
he sought refuge with the wild tribes
and asked if they had seen the blonde witch.
Indeed they had and gave him clues
of where she could be. He waited
until the ravenous swarm departed
and the sands stopped flying. He picked
some of the insects that had fallen
and ate a few before continuing his search
for the mother who had cursed him.

After many days of walking around
the Maratuja he came eye-to-eye
with his mother. 'Who is this
who interrupts Kelot and dares
look into her eyes?' barked
the woman. 'Mother, I am the son
you buried, but The Pigeons
saved me.' Kelot did not respond
she was mesmerised by his beauty.
Finally, she said as if to herself:
'He cannot be Damora's shit.
No, he can't, no he can't, he is…
he is beautiful like the winter moon.'
Jeremiah interrupted, 'Mother,
I forgive you for abandoning
and burying me
But I cannot pardon you
for cursing me. Please take away
my burden, I beg you.'
Kelot, spat three times,
slapped her son twice,
opened the bag she had hanging
from her neck and took out
a stick and hit her son's shoulders,
at the same time she chanted,
'Miru rutu puku ragu sutu
shica raca manu tera san dan.'

Jeremiah asked, 'Mother,
am I free of your curse?'
'Yes, son, now go, otherwise
I will put another curse on you.
Come back when the desert flowers
and the river flows out of its banks.'
'That will never happen,' Jeremiah said
and cried and this time his tears
turned to ashes like the fallen cities.

The Gone Days

Again and again, Jeremiah read
in the notebook that was amongst
the books he had found in the cave
in the Maratuja desert.
*'First came the fires, then the winds,
the constant tornadoes which
like a herd of camels destroyed
every blade of grass on the ground.
Buildings shook, crumpled and fell.
Cities, old and new disintegrated
like sand rocks, they turned to
a grey powder that choked humans
and beasts. No time to escape,
no time to hide. The Earth responded
to the cruel attacks, she cried
and rumbled and afterwards
tremors, eruptions, lava…then
silence…only the silence left.'*
Day after day Jeremiah pondered
the questions that haunted him
like the present is oppressed by the past.
Why had the books been burned?
Why was technology evil?
Why was it forbidden to talk about
life before the end of the old world?
The Pigeons had told him about
machines that could fly and think
but he was not to repeat this.

Jeremiah was not frightened
to use his reason so he promised
himself to find the answers.
He closed his eyes and sensed
the existence of the great consciousness
marooned in the infinite cosmos.
Its energy and light inspired his spirit.
Night slowly ascended like the birth
of Venus. The sky was now a black lace
embroidered with silver.
Hugging the notebook
he counted one hundred stars.
Tired he fell asleep and dreamt
that the answers to his questions
were hidden inside his head.

Jeremiah Was in the Dream of the Chaotic Minds

God-like geometry of complicated structures,
essential to his nature the need to know his mind.
Thoughts: particles in a ritual dance, which create
a reality and the necessity to embrace this world.
It is the imagined, quasi-divine world of the senses
where Jeremiah, in a casual way drowned his dreams
to destroy the desire to posses the sacred land,
to kill the ambition to dominate and to ignore
the pre-established ideologies.
This propelled him to an infinite regression
under the front step of his consciousness
covered by a subliminal shawl, then
he realised that he never stops dreaming.

Life in Epinaster

Parallel existences in a shared nightmare
pariahs of sombre and empty lives
isolated from each other and yet together.
Obtuse cacophony of their simple dreams
pathetic cadence of their love making murmurs
they are and they are not, in a virtual reality
of incongruent feelings. Pain and pleasure.
Two forces that repel and compel each other
two worlds that clash in space, elliptical orbits
that bring them to a forbidden ritual.
A distorted reality in their minds,
they travel through time and space.
Elementals, dreamers of dreams,
A sense of loss and an intense emptiness
pervade their beings and souls,
confusion, chaos, abashment,
entanglement of emotions. Solitude.
They are holograms, random shapes,
denizens, figures projected on a screen,
They are just survivors in a dead world
engaged in a charade of hollow feelings.

Humans

(After reading many of the books kept in the cave Jeremiah wrote in his notebook.)

Capable of the most honourable deeds
and the cruellest actions
contradictory beings –
creators of art and music yet
warmongers destroyers of lives,
builder of cities, gardens, parks…
effacers of forests and rivers
conservationists some, rapists others
philosophers and tyrants
free thinkers and demagogues
humanitarians and racists
scientists and murderers
All part of this mélange
we call the human race.

Graha

Jeremiah sat at the edge of the Lake Dead-no-Fish,
he wished for the moon and the stars to be reflected
on the dark waters like he had read in the books hidden
by the Pigeons in a cave in the Madura mountains.
'How lucky I am,' he thought and he named aloud
what made him fortunate, 'The Pigeons taught me to read,
they hid the books, I know now how the world was
before "wills" collided like the galaxies collide in the universe,
my mother rejected me but I am not a mutant bubbling curses.'
The young man stopped muttering when he heard a maiden
shouting for help. He stood up and at the top of his voice
asked what had scared such a fair maiden
like a deer being chased by a lion. 'What is a deer? A lion?'
she asked and continued, 'A ghost was chasing me.
I saw you and now I ask your protection,' saying this she fell
to her knees.
Jeremiah realised that he could not use the knowledge
gained from the cave books, as reading other than the code
was forbidden. 'There is no ghost following you. Rise maiden,'
he commanded and helped her stand up. Her perfume,
her skin and the tone of her voice made him want to make
love to her.
His whole body was begging make her yours, kiss her…
'I am Graha. There was a ghost but on seeing you it has
departed.'
With a trembling voice like the strings of a badly tuned sitar
he asked,
'Are you a virgin? Do you need a man to deflower you?'
'I am a virgin but my parents have sold me to the Great Code
Keeper.'

'Graha he is a man living just to dust flower vases.'
'He paid many Trunas for me, I obey so it is.'
'I'll walk you home,' he said grabbing her hand
and in his mind created fantasies, colourful as the pictures
in the pages with the secret knowledge. He left her.
Back at the lake he fell asleep he believed he was ice
in the morning he realised he was just water.

                                                                                           … He cried.

Versing in the Mind

Jeremiah fell sleep and entered a dream
of convoluted fantasy. He raised his eyes to the dark sky
where no stars shone or moon illuminated his path,
the proximity of the cosmos choked him with terror,
yet its energy and light made him discover the ethereal
and fragile silk which had been the work of a Bmori.
He wondered if he was awake, but no, it was a dream,
as real as his erection. Wrapped in fabric he was now
in flight, flapping invisible wings, then entered an obscure tunnel,
at its end sat a being with no head and a sword in his hand.
Was he a god? 'The Pigeons' had told him that no Gods
lived on earth or the heavens. He grabbed his genitals
because he knew the sword was to castrate him, he had not
coupled or procreated. He turned around and escaped
Thunder woke him up and Jeremiah remembered
the maiden of the lake. He wanted her, her hand to appease
his desire,
her voice to chant only for him, but she was promised,
her parents have sold her to the Great Code Keeper.

Jeremiah and Camus

Jeremiah lived
chained to a past
in a golden cage
his life an absent presence
which was like drowning
in a dry lake in one of
Jupiter'moons.

> He swam on sand
> flew on fire
> burned on sky.

Jeremiah wrote poems
to the gold that muted him
and his words became ashes
grey and black petals
like from the tree of death.

Jeremiah had read about Camus in one of the books in the cave, he thought he would like to talk to him and say: 'Albert, I am a prisoner of my own mind.' He imagined that Camus would have said: 'Embrace the absurd and search for meaning.'

The Genius and the Laurels

In the magical ceremony of a horizontal expansion,
the naked and the paradoxical, illuminated by the 'no reality'
and without prejudices, they submerged themselves
in the past, in a world without scruples or shame
at the margins of the senses. A foreigner, sceptical
with a false and sardonic laugh, gave Jeremiah the laurels.
The forces mixed with the proposed knowledge, plus
the uneasiness of the time, led to the revolt of the Vulgars.
They hollowed those who palpitated detaching the conscious 'I'.
Layers and more layers, of a superficial mentality,
 irreverent destroyers who transcended the ecstasies
and sublimated the sensations. Finally, they dressed in black
and departed. Jeremiah, his mind smoke and ashes,
embraced the ancestral fire of his genius
and decided to change his world.

Feeling

There they go, the suffering penitents
pious procession of the Mutants,
the dead but alive, there they go
praying to the non-existent gods
praying to the terracotta idols
that serve to hold their pain.
Jeremiah saw them from afar
and his heart trembled like the Earth
on the month the locust eat the wheat.

No, he did not fear or disliked the Mutants,
he wanted to tell them, 'If there were a god
the world would be as it was once.' He knew
that before the great tyrant there was
peace. Food and water were plentiful.
Machines flew, education was for all
and there were books: pieces of paper
glued together with symbols on them.

There were schools too. A place where
you could learn or discuss as the Pigeons do
who teach each other about the old world
before the destruction of the war of wars.
He felt his face wet and realised that
what he was feeling must have a name.
It was forbidden to talk or mix with the Mutants,
although he knew there was no god,
he ran and joined them, he cried no longer.

No Light

Far from everything, the ethereal now
where Jeremiah, imagined himself
fighting the forces of the present.
He asked himself a question, 'Why could I not
ignore the abuse and the deceit living life
as before, happy deflowering virgins?'
> *I could have answered you Jeremiah. You found*
> *those pieces of papers glued together,*
> *with symbols that made your synapses fire,*
> *those are books, treasures that opened your mind.*

He wanted the truth to be handed to all.
Digesting his anger, he prepared a speech
for the Great Code Keeper incinerator of knowledge,
his words a call to awaken the ignorant populace,
those who sell their daughters forced to procreate
those who despise The Mutants.
Perhaps I don't need words he thought
I need an army with guns and swords
but then, blood inundated his head, red to his core
he realised he was thinking like the people of the past
who killed not only lives but also hope. Embarrassed
he cried, kneeled on Mother Earth and kissed the ground
as the Pigeons had taught him when he had done wrong.
In a tenuous voice the young man asked for forgiveness.

The Woman

Obscurity of irreconcilable postulates,
discord and acrimony
scepticism veils his eyes…
Lord of Darkness bring Jeremiah to me
hear my wail, I pledge my allegiance,
give me his heart, I taught him to love.
In the sleepless nights I shout his name
while Damora enters me, hearing my call
he tears my flesh, he insults me
and covers me with spit. Do I care? No…

I hear my man spends his days deflowering virgins.
King of the Underworld I beg you,
make his member flaccid like wheat after the rains.

Famine

The Pigeons found Jeremiah the moment he imagined
he had a dog, the man from the past had written
about this faithful hairy being with four legs,
who did not speak but communicated. The small beast
ate meat as the humans did then. The Alpha Pigeon
pecked the now startled man and whispered,

'A famine will come. No food will grow for many moons,
the winds will come back, and the lands will dry again.
You need to prepare for what is to come. Plant corn
and tend the crop as we did for you. Collect mushrooms and seeds
to be kept in the cave. Many water bladders need to be filled.
Not a word to be said to anyone,' finished the Pigeon solemnly.
The One reflected and expressed his sorrow for other
humans, 'Why?
Why keep this knowledge secret? Don't others have the right
to know?'
Scratching the earth with one leg and moving one wing from
side to side
The bird explained, 'These beings are ignorant. They will believe
a warlock has spoken and will exile you to the Forbidden Lands.'
Jeremiah bowed to the Pigeon, who flew away,
sadness suffused his soul and body with the same intensity
as his desire to impregnate Graha. Head down,
dragging his feet he walked to the pine forest.

Jeremiah at the Edge of a Mountain

A swinging pendulum, the fall of a dice
what is on the side of what is normal?
What is an aberration? Rules admitted and manifested
in this land where incongruences and abuse are perpetrated
as the daily laments of the Code Keepers. Criminals…
are we infringing the law of nature? Coy solutions,
false perceptions and ignorance. Barbarisms postulated
by those who hold the power like misers hold their Trunas.
False ideas of a group of men who pray to an imaginary god
forcing women to procreate, making them slaves
of their body which are complete as Mother Earth was.
This won't make our land fertile, rivers won't overflow
with fish or the earth stop cracking and shaking.
By no fault of their own the Mutants are despised,
radiation and chemical warfare turned genes again and again
as we turn the corn to dry on their beds of banana leaves.
I know about genes, I read about them, they are
minuscule parts of our body which predict our future
like the witches do. The book in the cave said genes
were: *a distinct sequence of nucleotides forming
part of a chromosome*, but this I don't understand.

Graha's Hold

Graha knew Jeremiah would be by the river
many times, she had seen him there
sitting on a rock doing something
with a stick with which he scratched
on something that he holds with his other hand.
The young woman felt her heart beat
faster and faster as she approached the man.
She sat next to him and sighed, as a greeting
she said, 'Have the gods been good to you?'
'Now that you are here they have,' he replied
and quickly grabbed her hand which felt
like the newborn baby pigeons he used
to look after and play with when young.
'You have been on my mind longer
than our first meeting,' he whispered.
'Tell me, young breeder, how is that?'
'Many moons ago I discovered you were
a seller at the market. I often bought
corn for my parents just to see you,' he explained
as he hid his pencil and notebook.
'You are truly the child of the Pigeons?'
'Yes, I am indeed. They cared for me.'
'I am so sorry, a child with no parent.'
'Don't feel sorry for me maiden,
no human would have given me
what the Pigeons have, I honour
them, I protect them, and help them.'

Graha laughed and asked, 'How can
talking to feathered beings, be
better than those who give you life?'
'Maiden, they have given me life,
they saved me from death, they fed me
and gave me something that no one
in this forsaken village could. But let's
not talk about me. Would you like
to breathe good health in the Pine Forest?'
'I'd love that very much. Let me cover my face,
so no one sees me and run's to the Great Code
Keeper to tell him that his maiden was
cavorting with a young man,' and she laughed
as they run into the dark and humid solitary.

Respect

Graha and Jeremiah entered the pine forest
she took off her veil and smiled breathing the pure
and fresh air. 'Trees clean our air, we need to plant
trees, not breed humans,' said Jeremiah. Graha had heard
the people gossip at the market about the man
who had been raised by the Pigeons: the Evolved.
The plebs said he spoke of things they did not understand
but followed his advice because always brought good results.
The young woman knew he often uttered beautiful words.
She wanted to hear those sounds that brought joy to many,
so she pleaded with Jeremiah with one hand over her heart:
'Please, speak to me those words Epinasters beg you to say.'
'Maiden, those words are poetry, in ancient time it was said
that the gods spoke in poetry form. But let me look into your eyes,
because you inspire me,' Jeremiah held her face and kissed her,
like the Woman had taught him. The maiden trembled
as she felt his humid tongue enter her mouth. She pushed him
and with horror reflected on her expression softly asked:
'Are you trying to steal my spirit? You have scared me?'
'Graha, this is called a passionate kiss. I don't want to rob
your soul
I want to join it.' He brought her closer to his body and took
her hand
to his erect member. She did not complain and let him kiss her.
After they lay down on a pile of dry needles, The One recited
'The Marriage of Heaven and Hell' by Blake, one of his
favourite poems.

Graha's Prayer by the Lake

I want to believe what Jeremiah tells me:
'Humans are born to be free.' He proffers
solutions to our plight, he calls for democracy.
His words are as long as the Rock of Tears
and complicated as the baskets woven
by the Mutants. 'Trunas buy anything,'
he whispers in my ear, offering to buy me
from the Great Code Keeper, he wants me
to be like the eagles who no one can own.
I become frightened, as when the lights fall from the sky,
when with his magic stick, he copies nature,
on something he calls a 'notebook'. He plans
how to defeat my future master. Has the Woman,
who taught him to love, bewitched him again?
'If the town's people bestow me with power
I will free the Mutants and women, I'll allow the witches
to return to Epinaster, because they are medicine women
I will open schools and I will teach children to write,'
he says and his face reddens, and his body trembles.
Jeremiah does not only speak crazy words, he also speaks
beautiful words, he calls them poetry. He respects
what is preserved for my prospective owner,
but he does something with his tongue
 that makes me close my eyes and I reach the sky.

Gods of the above and of the underworld,
please I beg you, help me to understand him.

Pasodoble

Graha

Jeremiah may the gods smile at you
happy to see you at rest and alone
at the market people said you were sick
wrong they were health shines through your eyes young man.

Jeremiah

Graha my eyes shine because you are here.
But what brought you to me promised girl?
I also sought you but no good fortune
crossed my path and I returned to my cave.

Graha

I want to hear your words nights and days
no man in Epinaster is like you
you alone believe that we can be free
There is something that I want you to do.

Jeremiah

For you Graha I would plant and reap corn
for your parents I would tend goats
and collect mushrooms for the long dark days
but I would never give up my books.

Graha

Do you say that your heart holds love for me?
Would you be prepared to pierce a heart?
Can you hold a knife in your hand and kill?
Your words have taught me to dream of freedom.

Jeremiah

I am a man of honour and knowledge
to take a life is shameful and cruel.
Who is the one whose soul you want to free?
What pain or offense has this man caused you?

Graha

Like a goat I have been sold to this ogre,
soon the day of the wedding is coming
two full moons and I will be in his bed
and his fat ugly body will be on me.

Jeremiah

Now I know who you want out of the way
the Code Keeper who enslaves all of us
and whose life is ruled by Trunas and girls,
virgins who adorn his life as flowers.

What prize has he paid for you my dear girl?
Has he given Trunas to your parents?
Has he promised land at the birth of boys?
or simply has he threatened your parents?

Graha

The Code Keeper has paid many Trunas
more than all the fingers plus eight hands,
also my parents would move into his house
and all my sisters will marry his friends.

Jeremiah

He has paid ninety Trunas for you.
Maiden I can offer love and Trunas,
the Pigeons promised me rewards
because I love and serve them well always.

Graha

Will you buy me for love Jeremiah?
Will I be your slave and later sold?
Will you swap me for camels or horses?
Will you be kind or whip me for errors?

Jeremiah

All men and women are born to be free
violence is like a fire that eats the crops
it destroys and leaves useless ashes.
Words and Trunas always rule over knives.

I will buy you back and set you free
if you love me and want me for ever
I will treasure you and you will be my equal.
Say you love me and want to be with me.

Graha

Yes, I love you like plants love water
Yes, I love you like bats love dark nights
Yes, I love you like the locust love grasses
Yes, I love you like cacti love the heat.

Jeremiah Embarks on a Dangerous Affair

In the library in the cave, I found a book
about a revolution in the old kingdom of Egypt
Pepi II, the last Pharaoh of the 6th dynasty
who was overthrown by widespread popular uprising
Jack A. Goldstone, the writer of the book
was right when he said, 'Misery breeds revolt'
when oppression becomes too much to bear
the masses will rise against the oppressors.
I will discredit the Great Code Keeper
as well as his coterie, all abusers of power
exploiters of females, belittlers of the mutants,
denigrators of knowledge and technology.
What to do? How to do it? Who will help?
I need a plan on how to involve the people,
on how to enrage them and make them aware
of the injustices and suffering they face.

Planning the Revolution

I will dissolve the reign of the tyrants
I will reach the mind and heart of the oppressed
I will ignite the fervour for justice and equal rights
I will tell the people that freedom will gleam like a light
I will explain that we can succeed without violence.

Unity will be our shield
abuse will stop
courage must take a stand
justice will prevail.

I will instil in people the need to bring about change.
I will mobilise the witches, the mutants, the virgins and the slaves.
I will educate the groups about civil disobedience
I will explain non-violent methods of resistance.
I will teach about rights, democracy and technology.

We must be patient and persistent
change will happen
revolutions take time
we will win.

Jeremiah Asks the Pigeons For Their Blessing

Parents brothers and sisters
I stand here to tell you
that I am embarking
on a dangerous affair
I will start a revolution
against the Code Keepers
your support, your advice
and blessing I need.
You brought me up
loved and fed me,
taught me to read and
gave me the treasures
hidden in the cave.
I trust your knowledge,
please give me your approval.

The Pigeons Advise

Dear human son,
we know you will succeed
we will be here to assist you
now and after you gain control
we will influence people
while they are at rest or sleep
words in their ears will be spoken.
Hear our advice, starting a revolution
is a complex and dangerous endeavour
careful consideration must be given
to ethical and practical issues.
Here are some ideas that might help:
become a friend of the people
who work with the Code Keepers
gain their trust and raise their awareness
of their suffering and exploitation
do the same with the mutant and the witches
encourage disobedience and protests
educate all about their rights and democracy
and above all take measures to protect yourself.
Be patient and persistent in your efforts
revolutions take time, stay committed
we are here for you and always will.
educate all about their rights and democracy
and above all take measures to protect yourself.
Be patient and persistent in your efforts
revolutions take time, oh stay committed
we are here for you and always will.

The First Speech of Jeremiah

Hear me men and women of Epinaster I have words to tell you,
words that need to penetrate in your mind, and like you ponder on your dreams
ponder on my message. We live in a minute piece of land on a planet
which was once a garden but later destroyed, obliterated by ambition and greed.
Perhaps we are the last humans left who can build a better future.
We are forbidden to learn, to study, to create machines, why?
Just to keep us under control. The Code Keepers live in luxury,
demand the best of the crops, buy our women. We are slaves
to them and their code, let's free ourselves from their tyranny.
Brothers and sisters, we can build a future without doing more damage
to our dead rivers, our dry cracked land, our infertile soil
and sterile plants. Yes, our ancestors had machines, ate animals,
visited the moon and boiled the seas, we do not want to do the same.
Ignorance is like the borers that destroy our corn.
We can build machines to help us with our work,
we can learn how to clean our rivers and lakes
and perhaps dissipate the veil of clouds that obscure our days.
Hear me brothers and sisters, women are equal to men and
the Mutants deserve respect and may be cured.
The Witches know how to cure many the ill,
let them into our village with their idols, pots and drugs.
Books are not evil, books are children of the brain. Let's unite!
Let's create what is called democracy. No more Code Keepers,
no more elite, let's seek freedom as we seek mushrooms.

Let's unite! The Pigeons can educate everyone,
they have the knowledge of history and systems,
Free our women so they can be like the moon who
shows its face when she wants. If we unite I will start a school,
it will be like the sun which in the rare occasions shines for all.
Knowledge will destroy our apathy, let's follow the path of freedom
Yes, men and women of Epinaster, change, change is our mission.
Are you all with me? Are you Epinasters? Are you ready to be free?

Graha Escapes

Jeremiah

Graha what are you doing at this time of the night?

Graha

Jeremiah, I knew you would be here, I have escaped
your words have penetrated me like the roots penetrate the soil
I want to be free, I want to be yours and fight at your side
hide me in the cave until the right time comes.
Please take food to my parents and leave it at the entrance
of our humble dwelling. I have heard the people in town
they are all agree with your ideas. They are waiting for you
to tell them what to do. The Mutants believe you are a God.

Graha

Happiness you brought to my ears. You will be mine
and no one else's. I will do whatever you ask me.

Jeremiah

Let's walk to the cave there you will sleep in my arms
and if you wish it will be an honour for me to deflower you.

The Stone

A story written on an ancient stone
tells us about a man who changed the world
he had opened his mind to the oldest past
from there he learnt about evil and good.
With knowledge he defied those in power,
the Code and its Keepers were overthrown,
The Pigeons, faithful to their son
spread words that carried hope and trust.
Women grateful for their gains honoured him,
the Mutants, saved from their slavery,
swore allegiance to the brave young hero.
The town opened its gates to the banned witches,
who brought medicines and new ideas
to the ignorant populace.
The Code was destroyed and forgotten
the Code Keepers were forced to learn and to read.
Jeremiah, the visionary opened a school
a school where the Pigeons taught,
and a library with the books from the cave,
he named both after the man who owned the books.
Jeremiah married the maiden Graha
and until his death he taught love and kindness.

… And they made the same mistake again

www.ingramcontent.com/pod-product-compliance
Lightning Source LLC
Chambersburg PA
CBHW072137070526
44585CB00016B/1715